Art Nouveau Patterns

Marty Noble

Dover Publications, Inc.
Mineola, New York

Note

The Art Nouveau movement emerged during the Industrial Revolution of the late nineteenth century. The innovative ideas and cutting-edge technology of this modern age inspired artists to create the Art Nouveau style, a combination of asymmetrical ornamentation, sinuous lines, and organic forms. This new art form had a major impact on architecture, furniture, textiles, advertisements, jewelry, and many other items until the outbreak of World War I. The thirty allover patterns in this coloring book showcase a variety of Art Nouveau designs inspired by nature. There are exotic plants and flowers, foliage, birds, fish, floating swans, butterflies, and more—all accented with the curvilinear lines characteristic of the Art Nouveau style. Color the patterns anyway you like, but if you want an authentic Art Nouveau design use muted colors.

Bibliographical Note

Art Nouveau Patterns is a new work, first published by Dover Publications, Inc., in 2008.

DOVER *Pictorial Archive* SERIES

International Standard Book Number
ISBN-13: 978-0-486-46198-4
ISBN-10: 0-486-46198-X

Manufactured in the United States of America
Dover Publications, Inc., 31 East 2nd Street, Mineola, N.Y. 11501

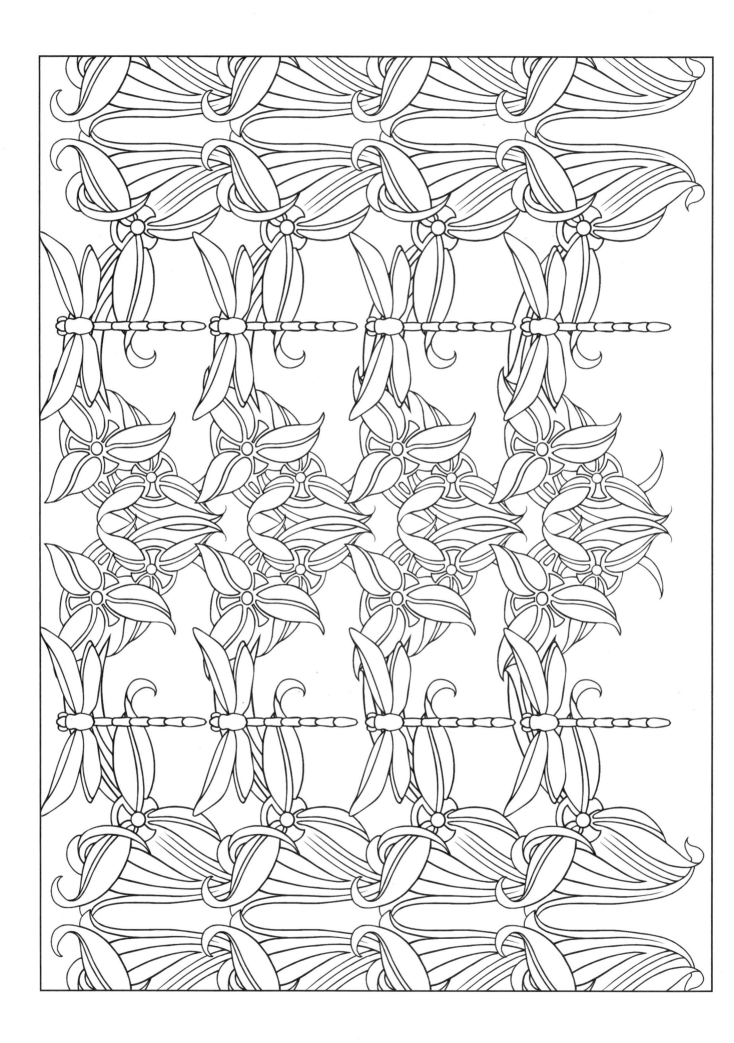

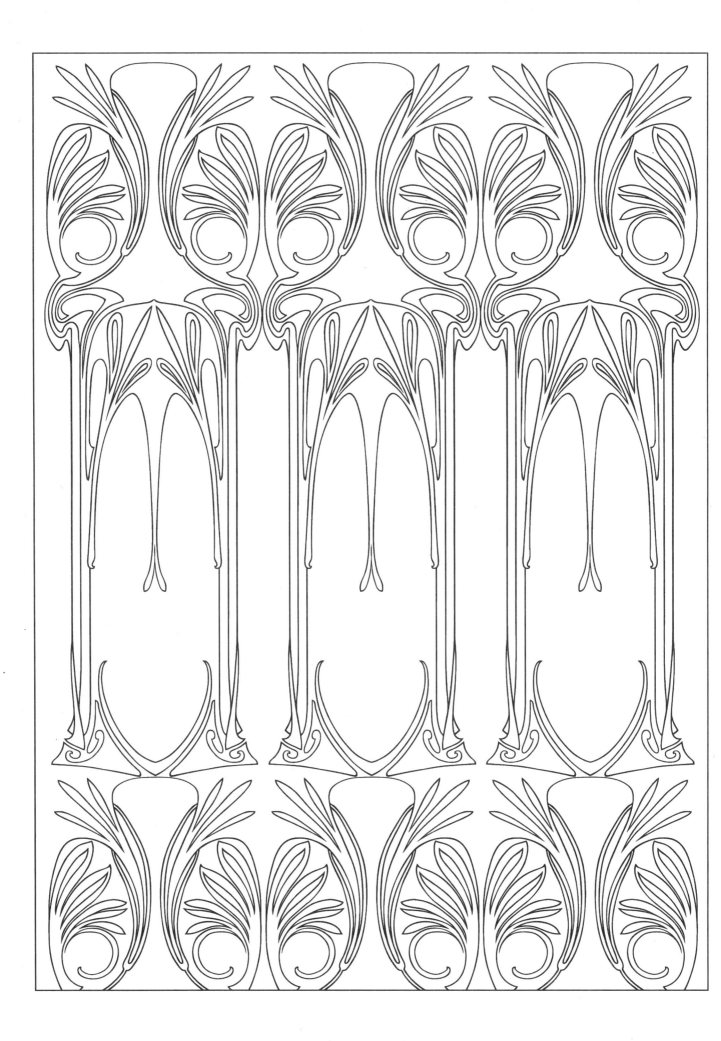